Microsoft Purview 101

The Microsoft Purview Companion Series

Dr. Patrick Jones

OLYMPUS ACADEMY
PRESS

TABLE OF CONTENTS

INTRODUCTION: WHY DATA SECURITY MATTERS IN THE MODERN WORKPLACE

Data is one of the most valuable assets an organization possesses. Whether it's financial records, customer information, employee data, or intellectual property, businesses rely on data to operate, innovate, and remain competitive. But with increasing digital transformation and remote collaboration, securing that data has never been more challenging.

Cyber threats are evolving at an alarming pace. Ransomware attacks, phishing scams, insider threats, and data breaches have become everyday risks for organizations of all sizes. Regulatory requirements like GDPR, HIPAA, and NIST add another layer of complexity, demanding that companies not only protect their data but also demonstrate compliance with strict security standards.

At the same time, employees expect to work from anywhere, share files seamlessly, and access the data they need in real time. Organizations must find a balance between keeping information secure and enabling a productive workforce. This is where Microsoft Purview comes into play—a powerful solution designed to help businesses protect, govern, and monitor their data across Microsoft 365 and beyond.

In the past, organizations focused on securing their corporate network with firewalls and access controls. But today, the traditional security perimeter is gone. Data flows across cloud services, mobile devices, and third-party applications, making it more difficult to track and control.

Some of the biggest security challenges organizations face today include:

- Increased cyber threats – Attackers use sophisticated techniques like ransomware, social engineering, and supply chain attacks to exploit security weaknesses.

- Insider risks – Employees and contractors with legitimate access to sensitive data can accidentally or intentionally cause data leaks.

- Regulatory compliance demands – Companies must prove they are handling data properly or risk fines and legal consequences.

- Remote and hybrid workforces – Employees expect to collaborate from anywhere, but security teams must ensure that data doesn't fall into the wrong hands.

These challenges make it impossible for IT teams to rely on manual security measures. Organizations need automated, AI-driven security solutions that can classify, protect, and monitor data in real time.

Microsoft Purview is an integrated suite of security, compliance, and data governance tools designed to help organizations:

- Classify and protect sensitive data using automated labeling and encryption.

- Enforce data loss prevention (DLP) policies to stop unauthorized sharing of confidential information.

- Detect insider risks and unusual activity before a security incident occurs.

- Meet compliance requirements with built-in regulatory tracking and audit capabilities.

Instead of using separate security tools for different risks, Purview provides a centralized approach to data protection—making it easier for organizations to enforce security policies without disrupting employee productivity.

This book is designed for security professionals, IT administrators, and business leaders who want to learn how to implement Microsoft Purview to strengthen their organization's data security and compliance.

The book is structured to guide you through:

- Understanding Microsoft Purview's core features and how they address modern security challenges.
- Setting up and configuring security policies to protect sensitive data across Microsoft 365.
- Using AI-driven tools to automate threat detection and compliance management.
- Applying real-world strategies to prevent data loss, insider threats, and regulatory violations.

By the end of this book, you will have a clear roadmap for implementing Microsoft Purview in your organization, ensuring that your data is secure, compliant, and properly governed.

To make these concepts easier to understand, each chapter will include a real-world scenario featuring Alex, an IT security professional working at a growing technology firm.

Alex's company has recently experienced a security scare—a confidential financial report was mistakenly emailed to an external recipient. While the company avoided serious consequences, the incident revealed gaps in their security policies and made leadership realize that they needed a stronger data protection strategy.

As Alex learns to implement Microsoft Purview, data loss prevention policies, insider risk management, and AI-driven security automation, you will follow along and see how these solutions apply in real business scenarios.

Through Alex's journey, you'll gain practical insights into how Microsoft Purview can be used to prevent data leaks, improve compliance, and secure sensitive information.

Data security is no longer just an IT concern—it is a business necessity. Organizations that fail to secure their data risk financial losses, regulatory fines, and reputational damage.

Microsoft Purview provides the tools needed to classify, protect, and monitor sensitive data, but success depends on how organizations implement and manage these security policies.

With the right strategy, businesses can protect their data, enable secure collaboration, and meet compliance requirements—all without disrupting productivity.

As we move into Chapter 1, we'll start by understanding Microsoft Purview's core security and compliance features and why it plays a critical role in today's evolving security landscape.

CHAPTER 1: UNDERSTANDING MICROSOFT PURVIEW – THE FOUNDATION OF DATA SECURITY

Data security is one of the most pressing concerns for modern organizations. The days of relying on network firewalls and on-premises security controls are over. As businesses continue to move to the cloud, share data across multiple platforms, and allow employees to work remotely, the challenge of securing sensitive information has never been greater.

Microsoft Purview was designed to address these challenges by providing a comprehensive security, compliance, and risk management solution that allows organizations to discover, classify, protect, and govern their data—no matter where it resides. Instead of relying on fragmented security tools, Microsoft Purview unifies data security, compliance, and risk mitigation into a single platform, making it easier for IT and security teams to gain visibility and control over their sensitive information.

Data security is no longer just an IT issue—it's a business imperative. Organizations that fail to protect their data risk financial losses, reputational damage, and regulatory penalties. But security isn't just about preventing breaches; it's also about enabling secure collaboration, ensuring compliance, and maintaining trust. This is where Microsoft Purview plays a vital role.

Microsoft Purview is an end-to-end security, compliance, and data governance platform designed to help organizations:

- Identify and classify sensitive data across Microsoft 365, Azure, and third-party environments.
- Enforce security policies that prevent data leaks, unauthorized access, and insider threats.

- Monitor and investigate security incidents with advanced auditing and risk management tools.

- Ensure regulatory compliance by aligning with GDPR, HIPAA, NIST, and other data protection standards.

- Automate security processes to improve efficiency and reduce the burden on IT and security teams.

Instead of treating security and compliance as separate concerns, Purview brings them together under one unified framework. This holistic approach allows organizations to maintain strong security controls while enabling employees to work efficiently without unnecessary restrictions.

Microsoft Purview consists of several integrated security and compliance solutions that work together to protect data, prevent security incidents, and maintain compliance.

- Data Classification & Sensitivity Labels: Automatically classify and tag documents, emails, and cloud storage data based on sensitivity.

- Data Loss Prevention (DLP): Prevent employees from accidentally or intentionally sharing sensitive information through email, OneDrive, or Teams.

- Insider Risk Management: Detect unusual data access behavior and prevent insider threats before they escalate.

- Information Protection & Encryption: Apply encryption policies to protect confidential files—even when shared externally.

- Compliance Manager & Regulatory Readiness: Measure and track compliance with industry regulations and automatically generate reports.

Each of these tools plays a critical role in securing an organization's data, but the true power of Purview comes from its seamless integration with Microsoft 365 and Azure, allowing organizations to apply consistent security policies across their entire environment.

Microsoft Purview is used across various industries and business scenarios to address a wide range of security and compliance challenges.

- A financial services company needs to prevent unauthorized access to customer financial data. Purview's DLP policies automatically block employees from emailing sensitive financial records to personal accounts.

- A healthcare provider must comply with HIPAA regulations. Purview ensures that patient records remain encrypted and protected at all times.

- A technology company struggles with insider threats—employees downloading proprietary data before leaving the company. Insider Risk Management detects this behavior and alerts security teams before data is leaked.

- A remote workforce introduces security challenges for a global enterprise. Purview monitors and restricts data access on unmanaged devices to prevent leaks.

- A legal firm needs to ensure that confidential case files remain secure. Information Protection and encryption ensure that only authorized users can access legal documents.

These real-world examples show how Microsoft Purview helps organizations reduce security risks while maintaining compliance and enabling secure collaboration.

Alex's Journey: Understanding Why His Company Needs Purview

Alex, a security specialist at a mid-sized technology firm, had always assumed that his company's data security policies were strong enough. But after an employee mistakenly emailed a confidential client contract to the wrong recipient, the IT team realized that they lacked visibility and control over sensitive information.

After evaluating several security solutions, Alex recommended Microsoft Purview to centralize and automate data security policies. He quickly identified several critical weaknesses in his company's current security posture:

- They had no way of knowing where sensitive data was stored. Documents containing confidential information were scattered across email, SharePoint, and OneDrive, making it difficult to enforce protection policies.

- Employees were sharing data without restrictions. There were no controls in place to prevent accidental leaks or unauthorized file sharing.

- Security incidents were hard to track. If an employee accessed or modified a sensitive file, there was no audit trail to determine who made the change or when it occurred.

Alex's first step was to gain executive buy-in for Microsoft Purview. He explained that without proper data classification, sensitivity labels, and access controls, the company was at risk of security breaches and compliance violations. He also demonstrated how Purview's automated security features would reduce the workload on IT while improving overall security.

Once he had approval, Alex began configuring Purview's security policies, starting with sensitivity labels and Data Loss Prevention (DLP). He worked with department heads to identify which types of data needed the highest level of protection, ensuring that security policies aligned with business needs.

Within weeks, his company saw immediate improvements. Employees no longer had to guess whether a document was safe to share—Purview automatically applied the appropriate security policies. IT had full visibility into how sensitive data was being accessed, shared, and stored.

Alex quickly realized that implementing Microsoft Purview was about more than just compliance—it was about enabling the company to operate securely without disrupting productivity. The journey was just beginning, but he knew that this was the foundation of a strong security strategy.

Understanding Microsoft Purview is the first step toward building a more secure and compliant organization. Data security is not just about preventing attacks—it's about proactively managing risks, enforcing policies, and maintaining trust.

With Purview, organizations gain the ability to classify, protect, and monitor their data at scale. By implementing sensitivity labels, DLP policies, and insider risk management, businesses can prevent security incidents before they happen.

As Alex continued learning about Purview's capabilities, he realized that security is not just about tools—it's about creating a security-first culture. In the next chapter, he would take the next step: configuring Microsoft Purview and setting up security policies for his organization.

CHAPTER 2: SETTING UP MICROSOFT PURVIEW FOR YOUR ORGANIZATION

Implementing a security and compliance solution like Microsoft Purview is not just about turning on features. It requires careful planning, the right licensing, and a clear understanding of how to configure policies that align with an organization's security needs. Without the proper setup, security gaps can emerge, leaving sensitive data vulnerable to leaks, insider threats, or regulatory non-compliance.

Before diving into advanced features like sensitivity labels and insider risk management, organizations must start with the foundational setup. This includes ensuring that the correct licensing is in place, assigning appropriate access roles, navigating the Microsoft Purview Compliance Portal, and configuring core security settings.

For many IT teams, the initial setup of a security platform can feel overwhelming, but Microsoft Purview is designed to be both comprehensive and user-friendly. By following a structured approach, organizations can set up a strong security framework that supports long-term data protection.

The first step in setting up Microsoft Purview is ensuring that the organization has the correct licenses. Not all security and compliance features are available in every Microsoft 365 plan, and using Purview effectively requires the right level of access.

Microsoft offers different security and compliance capabilities depending on the licensing tier. Organizations using Microsoft 365 E3 have access to core features like data classification and sensitivity labels, but more advanced security controls, such as insider risk management and advanced auditing, require an upgrade to Microsoft 365 E5. For companies that do not want a full E5 license, Microsoft offers standalone compliance add-ons to extend Purview's functionality.

Equally important is assigning the right roles and permissions within the Purview Compliance Portal. Not every IT administrator or security analyst needs full access, and role-based access control helps maintain security while ensuring that only authorized users can manage policies and review compliance reports. The key roles within Purview include the compliance administrator, who has full access to security and compliance settings; the security administrator, who manages security policies; and the compliance data administrator, who oversees data classification and retention policies. By carefully defining access levels, organizations can enforce security while reducing the risk of accidental misconfigurations.

Once licensing and access roles are in place, the next step is to familiarize key stakeholders with the Microsoft Purview Compliance Portal. This is the central hub where organizations can configure policies, monitor security incidents, and track compliance status.

The Purview portal is designed to bring together all aspects of data security, compliance, and risk management under one interface. The dashboard provides visibility into sensitive data exposure, compliance risks, and insider threats, allowing security teams to quickly identify areas that need attention.

To begin configuring Purview, administrators should start by exploring key areas of the portal:

- Data classification, where sensitivity labels and data loss prevention policies are managed
- Information protection, which controls encryption and access restrictions
- Compliance manager, which helps organizations track regulatory compliance requirements
- Insider risk management, which provides visibility into potential security threats from within the organization

By taking time to understand the layout of the Purview Compliance Portal, security teams can ensure that they are using its full capabilities to protect the organization's data.

Configuring Microsoft Purview goes beyond initial access and navigation. The true value of the platform comes from its ability to enforce security and compliance policies that align with an organization's needs.

One of the first policies to set up is sensitivity labels. These labels allow organizations to classify data based on confidentiality levels, applying automatic encryption or access restrictions to prevent unauthorized sharing. Setting up these labels involves defining classification categories, such as internal use, confidential, and highly confidential, and applying them to emails, documents, and SharePoint content.

Alongside sensitivity labels, organizations should configure data loss prevention policies. These policies monitor and restrict the transmission of sensitive information, preventing employees from emailing confidential files to personal accounts or uploading them to unauthorized cloud storage services. By setting up predefined DLP rules, security teams can enforce data protection without relying on manual oversight.

Retention policies are another critical aspect of Purview's setup. Different industries have varying requirements for how long certain types of data must be stored before deletion. By configuring retention policies within Purview, organizations can ensure that documents and emails are preserved for legal or compliance reasons while automatically removing data that is no longer needed.

Access controls should also be considered during the initial setup. Organizations using Microsoft 365 and Purview should align their security settings with a zero trust model, ensuring that employees and third parties only have access to the data necessary for their role. Conditional access policies can restrict access to sensitive data based on factors such as user identity, device security status, and geographic location.

Alex's Journey: Getting Access and Exploring the Compliance Portal

After convincing leadership to implement Microsoft Purview, Alex quickly realized that getting started required more than just flipping a switch. His first challenge was ensuring that the company had the correct licensing in place. His organization was using Microsoft 365 E3, but he soon discovered that some of the security features they needed, such as insider risk management, were only available in E5. After discussions with IT leadership, the company decided to purchase a compliance add-on rather than upgrading every user to E5.

With licensing secured, Alex moved on to assigning access roles. He didn't want every IT administrator to have full control over security settings, so he carefully designated compliance administrators and security analysts based on their responsibilities. He also assigned read-only roles to legal and HR teams that needed access to compliance reports but didn't require the ability to modify policies.

Once access roles were finalized, Alex logged into the Microsoft Purview Compliance Portal for the first time. The dashboard provided an overview of the company's current security status, highlighting areas where data was at risk. He took time to explore the portal, reviewing features such as data classification, information protection, and compliance manager. As he navigated through the settings, he began formulating a plan for how to structure sensitivity labels and DLP policies.

His first major task was setting up the company's initial sensitivity labels. After consulting with department heads, he created three core classifications: public, internal, and confidential. He then configured encryption policies to automatically apply when documents were labeled as confidential, ensuring that only authorized employees could access them.

Over the next few weeks, Alex worked with IT and security teams to configure additional Purview features, including data loss prevention policies that restricted sharing of customer information outside the company. He also implemented retention policies for financial and legal documents to meet compliance requirements.

As Alex became more familiar with Purview, he realized that setting up security policies was not a one-time event. The company would need to continuously review and adjust policies as threats evolved and compliance requirements changed. But with Purview in place, they now had the tools to enforce security and compliance with greater efficiency than ever before.

Setting up Microsoft Purview is a foundational step in protecting an organization's data. Without proper licensing, access controls, and security policies, sensitive information can remain vulnerable to unauthorized access and accidental leaks. By taking the time to configure sensitivity labels, data loss prevention, and retention policies, organizations can establish a strong security framework that aligns with their business needs.

As Alex learned, navigating the Microsoft Purview Compliance Portal and structuring security policies takes time, but the long-term benefits far outweigh the initial setup effort. With the right approach, organizations can ensure that Purview becomes an integral part of their security and compliance strategy, providing ongoing protection as data security threats continue to evolve.

CHAPTER 3: INFORMATION PROTECTION BASICS – HOW MICROSOFT PURVIEW SECURES DATA

In today's digital landscape, data security is about more than just keeping hackers out of corporate systems. Organizations must ensure that sensitive information remains protected no matter where it is stored, how it is shared, or who accesses it. With employees working remotely, collaborating across departments, and sharing files across multiple platforms, the challenge of keeping data secure while maintaining productivity has never been greater.

Microsoft Purview provides a comprehensive approach to information protection by allowing organizations to classify, label, and encrypt sensitive data automatically. With built-in integration across Microsoft 365, Purview ensures that security policies apply consistently, whether data is stored in emails, documents, or cloud-based collaboration tools like SharePoint and Teams.

To effectively safeguard corporate data, IT and security teams must understand how Microsoft Purview classifies data, how sensitivity labels and encryption work, and how these measures integrate with broader security tools like Microsoft Defender. Establishing these foundational security controls is essential for preventing data leaks, maintaining compliance, and enabling employees to work securely.

Before implementing Microsoft Purview's information protection features, organizations must first understand the core principles of securing data: data classification, sensitivity labeling, and encryption. Each of these plays a critical role in defining how information is protected.

Data classification is the process of categorizing information based on its sensitivity and importance. Organizations handle a wide range of data types, from general business documents to highly confidential financial or legal records. By classifying this data, businesses can enforce security policies tailored to different levels of risk.

For example, a company might classify its data into the following categories:

- Public – Information that can be shared openly, such as marketing brochures and publicly available reports.

- Internal Only – Data that is restricted to company employees but does not contain highly sensitive information.

- Confidential – Documents that contain business-sensitive information, such as financial reports or internal strategy documents.

- Highly Confidential – Data that, if exposed, could cause significant harm to the company, such as customer personal information, employee records, or intellectual property.

Once data classification policies are in place, organizations can apply sensitivity labels to ensure that files and emails are automatically protected according to their classification.

Sensitivity labels allow security teams to enforce rules that dictate how a file can be accessed, shared, and stored. Labels can be applied manually by users or automatically based on pre-defined conditions, such as the presence of credit card numbers or confidential keywords.

For instance, an email labeled Highly Confidential could be configured to:

- Encrypt the message to ensure only authorized recipients can open it.

- Prevent forwarding or copying to stop unintended sharing.

- Apply a watermark indicating that the content is sensitive.

Encryption plays a crucial role in information protection by ensuring that only authorized users can access and read sensitive data. Even if an attacker intercepts an encrypted file, they will not be able to decrypt it without the appropriate credentials.

Microsoft Purview uses Azure Information Protection (AIP) encryption to safeguard sensitive files. This ensures that data remains protected even when shared externally. Unlike traditional access control measures, which only protect data inside corporate systems, encryption secures information throughout its entire lifecycle—whether it's stored in OneDrive, shared in an email, or downloaded onto a local device.

Sensitivity labels provide organizations with a powerful tool for managing information security across Microsoft 365. Once labels are applied, they enforce security policies that follow the document wherever it goes.

Administrators can configure sensitivity labels to:

- Encrypt documents and emails to prevent unauthorized access.

- Restrict sharing to specific individuals or groups within the organization.

- Apply visual markings, such as headers and watermarks, to indicate sensitivity levels.

- Control file permissions, limiting who can edit, print, or copy a document.

- Automatically apply labels based on content detection, such as financial data or personally identifiable information (PII).

For example, if an employee creates a spreadsheet containing customer Social Security numbers, Microsoft Purview can automatically apply a Confidential label, encrypt the file, and prevent external sharing. This removes the burden on employees to manually classify documents while ensuring that security policies are enforced consistently.

While Microsoft Purview focuses on preventing data leaks and enforcing compliance policies, Microsoft Defender enhances security by detecting and responding to threats that could compromise sensitive information. The integration between Purview and Defender provides organizations with a layered security approach that combines proactive data protection with advanced threat detection.

Microsoft Defender for Office 365 helps prevent phishing attacks and malicious email threats that could lead to unauthorized access to sensitive data. By analyzing email patterns and detecting suspicious activity, Defender can block phishing attempts before they reach employees.

Microsoft Defender for Endpoint adds another layer of security by monitoring endpoint devices for suspicious behavior. If an employee's device is compromised, Defender can isolate it from the network, preventing the spread of malware and protecting sensitive files stored locally.

By integrating Purview's information protection capabilities with Defender's threat detection tools, organizations can ensure that data security policies are enforced proactively while responding quickly to emerging threats.

Alex's Journey: Setting Up Sensitivity Labels for His Organization

After successfully setting up Microsoft Purview's security framework, Alex turned his attention to one of the most critical aspects of data protection: sensitivity labels. His company had suffered a minor but alarming security incident when an employee mistakenly emailed confidential financial reports to an external vendor without realizing the sensitivity of the information.

Determined to prevent similar incidents, Alex began working on a sensitivity labeling strategy that would automate security enforcement without disrupting productivity.

His first step was to define classification levels based on the company's needs. He worked closely with HR, finance, and legal teams to identify which types of data required the highest level of protection. Together, they created four core labels:

- Public – No restrictions, available for external sharing.

- Internal Only – Restricted to employees, with no external sharing allowed.

- Confidential – Encrypted automatically, limited to specific teams.

- Highly Confidential – Encrypted, blocked from being emailed externally, and watermarked for visibility.

With classification levels finalized, Alex configured auto-labeling rules to ensure that files containing sensitive keywords—such as "confidential," "financial report," or "SSN"—were automatically labeled and secured.

Once the sensitivity labels were in place, Alex conducted a training session for employees to help them understand how data protection policies worked. He reassured them that the new security measures would not slow down their work but would instead help prevent accidental data leaks.

Over the next month, Alex noticed a significant improvement in how data was handled across the organization. Employees became more aware of security policies, sensitive files were automatically encrypted, and unauthorized sharing attempts were blocked.

By implementing sensitivity labels and encryption policies within Microsoft Purview, Alex helped his company achieve a higher level of data security while maintaining compliance with industry regulations.

Data security is about more than just preventing cyberattacks—it's about ensuring that sensitive information remains protected at all times. By classifying data, applying sensitivity labels, and encrypting confidential files, organizations can proactively safeguard their information against both internal and external threats.

Microsoft Purview makes it easy for companies to implement these security measures without disrupting productivity. With sensitivity labels and data loss prevention policies in place, organizations can enforce consistent security policies across Microsoft 365, ensuring that sensitive information stays protected no matter where it travels.

As Alex prepared for his next challenge, he knew that securing data was only one part of the equation. His next task was to implement Data Loss Prevention (DLP) policies to prevent unauthorized data sharing—a step that would further strengthen his organization's overall security posture.

CHAPTER 4: IMPLEMENTING DATA LOSS PREVENTION (DLP) WITH PURVIEW

Every organization handles sensitive data, whether it's customer information, financial records, healthcare data, or intellectual property. While security policies and employee training can reduce the risk of data exposure, mistakes still happen. An employee might email a confidential report to the wrong recipient, upload a sensitive file to personal cloud storage, or copy proprietary data onto a USB drive. In some cases, insiders may intentionally try to remove or share data for malicious purposes.

This is where Microsoft Purview's Data Loss Prevention (DLP) capabilities come in. DLP policies are designed to detect, monitor, and prevent the unauthorized sharing of sensitive information, ensuring that organizations can enforce data protection without relying on manual oversight.

Microsoft Purview provides organizations with the ability to automate data loss prevention, applying policies across emails, cloud storage, and even Microsoft Teams. By defining rules for how data can be accessed and shared, security teams can significantly reduce the risk of accidental leaks and insider threats while maintaining compliance with regulatory requirements.

Data Loss Prevention is a security framework that helps organizations protect sensitive data by enforcing rules on how it can be shared, transferred, or stored. The goal of DLP is to ensure that confidential information does not leave the organization in an unauthorized or insecure way.

Many industries have strict regulatory requirements that mandate the protection of sensitive data. For example, financial institutions must comply with regulations like PCI-DSS to protect credit card information, while healthcare organizations must follow HIPAA to safeguard patient records. A robust DLP strategy helps businesses meet these legal obligations while also preventing costly data breaches and reputational damage.

DLP policies can be configured to automatically detect and respond to security risks in real time. For example:

- Blocking an email that contains sensitive customer data from being sent to an external domain

- Preventing employees from copying confidential documents to USB drives or unauthorized cloud services

- Alerting security teams when a large volume of sensitive files is downloaded within a short period

By implementing DLP policies, organizations gain greater visibility into how data is being used and can take proactive steps to prevent security incidents.

Setting up DLP policies in Microsoft Purview requires defining which data should be protected, where the policies should be applied, and what actions should be taken when a policy is violated.

The first step in configuring DLP policies is identifying which types of sensitive information need protection. Microsoft Purview comes with built-in policy templates that help organizations detect and safeguard sensitive data types, such as:

- Personally identifiable information (PII), including Social Security numbers, passport numbers, and driver's license numbers

- Financial data, such as credit card and bank account numbers

- Healthcare-related information protected under HIPAA regulations

- Confidential business data, including trade secrets, internal financial reports, and intellectual property

Organizations can also create custom policies based on their specific needs. For instance, a law firm may need to prevent the sharing of client case files, while a technology company might want to restrict access to product development documents.

Once the types of sensitive data are identified, the next step is determining where the DLP policies should be enforced. Microsoft Purview allows organizations to apply DLP rules to:

- Exchange Online (emails)

- SharePoint and OneDrive (documents and files)

- Microsoft Teams (chats and shared files)

- Endpoint devices (laptops, desktops, and mobile devices)

For example, a company may create a policy that prevents employees from sending emails containing credit card numbers outside the organization. If an employee attempts to send such an email, the DLP policy can block the message, notify the sender, and alert IT security.

Similarly, an organization can prevent employees from uploading sensitive documents to personal cloud storage, such as Google Drive or Dropbox. If an attempt is made, the file transfer can be blocked, and the user can receive a warning message explaining why the action is restricted.

DLP policies are not just about detecting violations; they also automate enforcement actions to minimize security risks. Organizations can configure policies to:

- Block actions immediately (e.g., stopping an email from being sent)

- Warn users before they complete an action, giving them a chance to reconsider

- Log incidents for security teams to review without interrupting user workflows

For example, a company might allow employees to share sensitive financial data internally but block it from being emailed externally. If an employee attempts to email an external recipient, they receive a notification that the email violates security policies, and the email is automatically blocked.

These automated enforcement actions reduce human error and ensure that security policies are consistently applied across the organization.

DLP policies are especially useful in preventing common data security incidents that organizations face every day.

A finance department employee drafts an email containing an Excel file with confidential customer payment details. The employee accidentally enters the wrong recipient's email address—an external vendor instead of an internal team member.

Microsoft Purview detects that the attachment contains sensitive financial data, blocks the email from being sent, and alerts the employee with a message explaining why the action was prevented. The employee realizes their mistake and corrects the recipient before resending.

A remote worker attempts to upload a confidential HR file containing employee salaries to their personal OneDrive account so they can work on it later. A DLP policy detects that the document contains protected HR data, automatically stops the upload, and sends a security alert to the IT team.

By enforcing this policy, the organization prevents sensitive employee data from being stored in an unauthorized location, reducing the risk of exposure.

An employee who has recently resigned begins downloading large volumes of confidential company data from SharePoint. A DLP policy detects the unusual activity, generates an alert for the security team, and automatically revokes the employee's access to sensitive files.

By catching this behavior early, the organization prevents data exfiltration before it becomes a full-blown security breach.

Alex's Journey: Protecting Sensitive Data with DLP

After implementing sensitivity labels and encryption policies, Alex's next priority was setting up data loss prevention policies to prevent sensitive information from leaving the organization.

The wake-up call came when the company's CFO received an email from a vendor claiming they had never received an invoice. Upon investigation, Alex discovered that an employee had sent the invoice to the wrong external recipient. While the mistake was unintentional, it raised concerns about how easily sensitive financial data could be shared without security controls in place.

Determined to prevent similar incidents, Alex began working on DLP policies tailored to his company's needs. He started by identifying the most sensitive data categories, including:

- Employee personal information
- Customer financial records
- Confidential legal contracts

He then configured DLP rules that prevented these data types from being shared externally via email, uploaded to personal cloud storage, or copied to USB drives.

Once the policies were in place, he ran tests to see how they would behave in real-world scenarios. In one test, an employee tried sending an email containing credit card numbers to an external partner. The email was automatically blocked, and the employee received a notification explaining why.

After refining the policies based on feedback, Alex provided training sessions for employees to ensure they understood the new security measures. He explained that DLP policies weren't meant to restrict productivity but to safeguard sensitive data from being exposed accidentally.

Over time, data leaks became far less frequent, and employees became more cautious about how they handled sensitive information. With DLP policies in place, the company now had greater confidence in its ability to protect critical business data.

Implementing Data Loss Prevention is a crucial step in securing an organization's information. By automating the detection and prevention of unauthorized data sharing, DLP policies help businesses minimize the risk of data breaches and compliance violations.

For Alex, setting up DLP was a turning point in his company's security strategy. But he knew there was still more to do. His next challenge was detecting and managing insider threats—a task that would require Microsoft Purview's Insider Risk Management tools.

CHAPTER 5: UNDERSTANDING INSIDER RISK AND DATA SECURITY MONITORING

Protecting an organization's data isn't just about stopping cybercriminals from breaking in. Some of the biggest risks come from inside the company itself. Employees, contractors, and even executives all have access to sensitive information, and while most people act in good faith, mistakes happen. Even worse, some insiders intentionally try to steal or leak data.

Insider threats fall into two main categories: unintentional mistakes and malicious actions. An employee might accidentally send confidential client information to the wrong recipient, or they might download company documents to a personal device without realizing the security implications. In more serious cases, an insider might steal intellectual property before leaving for a competitor or attempt to sell sensitive data to an external party.

Because insider threats often involve individuals with legitimate access to company systems, they can be difficult to detect. This is where Microsoft Purview's Insider Risk Management tools come in. By monitoring activity patterns and detecting unusual behavior, organizations can proactively identify risks, investigate suspicious actions, and prevent data leaks before they happen.

Not all insider threats are deliberate, and understanding the difference between negligence and malicious intent is critical for implementing an effective insider risk strategy.

Most employees don't mean to cause harm, but human error is one of the biggest contributors to data breaches. Some of the most common mistakes include:

- Emailing the wrong recipient – An employee accidentally sends a confidential document to a competitor with a similar email address.

- Uploading sensitive files to personal cloud storage – An employee working remotely stores company data on Google Drive instead of the company's OneDrive.

- Downloading files to unsecured devices – An employee transfers internal reports to a personal USB drive, which later gets lost or stolen.

- Weak passwords and credential sharing – A user shares their login details with a colleague, unintentionally allowing unauthorized access to sensitive files.

These mistakes may not be malicious, but they can still lead to regulatory fines, reputational damage, and financial loss. Organizations must have security policies and training in place to prevent unintentional insider risks.

Unlike accidental threats, malicious insiders knowingly violate security policies to steal, leak, or sabotage company data. Some common scenarios include:

- Data theft before resignation – An employee planning to leave the company downloads confidential client lists or product designs for use at a competitor.

- Selling or leaking sensitive data – An insider with financial motives steals proprietary information and sells it on the dark web.

- Disruptive sabotage – A disgruntled employee deletes critical files or corrupts databases to harm the company.

Malicious insiders often try to cover their tracks, making it harder to detect their activities. Security teams need real-time monitoring and automated alerts to recognize unusual behavior before damage is done.

Microsoft Purview provides Insider Risk Management tools that help organizations detect risky behaviors, analyze security incidents, and take preventative action before data is lost. Instead of simply reacting to security breaches, Purview allows security teams to proactively identify potential insider threats.

Purview Insider Risk Management continuously scans for suspicious user activities, such as:

- Unusual file downloads – A user suddenly downloads thousands of files from SharePoint.

- Data transfers to external accounts – A sensitive financial document is uploaded to an unauthorized personal email address.

- Unusual login attempts – A company executive's credentials are used from a new location or device.

- Repeated policy violations – A user repeatedly ignores security warnings about sharing confidential documents.

When Purview detects a pattern of risky behavior, it generates an insider risk alert that can be reviewed by security teams. The system does not assume guilt but instead provides contextual information, allowing security teams to investigate further.

To reduce false positives and ensure only relevant activities trigger alerts, organizations can customize risk detection policies. Some best practices include:

- Defining risk indicators – Organizations can set specific rules to monitor activities like excessive file downloads, frequent access to confidential data, or login attempts from unapproved locations.

- Establishing user risk scoring – Instead of treating all security alerts the same way, Purview assigns risk scores based on the severity of behavior. For example, a user who downloads one confidential document might trigger a minor alert, while someone copying an entire database would be flagged as a high-risk event.

- Integrating with HR policies – Organizations can align Purview alerts with HR and legal policies, ensuring that security teams take appropriate action in compliance with internal guidelines.

By creating customized insider risk policies, organizations can focus on real threats while minimizing unnecessary alerts.

When an insider risk alert is triggered, security teams need to review the event, gather evidence, and determine the appropriate response. Microsoft Purview makes this process easier by providing detailed activity logs, risk timelines, and automated response options.

Key Investigation Steps

1. Review the alert – Security teams analyze the details of the flagged activity, such as file names, timestamps, and user actions.

2. Assess intent – Was this an accidental policy violation or an intentional act? Security teams look for patterns in user behavior.

3. Take action – Depending on the severity, organizations can choose to:

   o Warn the user – If the action was accidental, the employee receives a security notification.

   o Restrict access – If an employee is at high risk, their account access can be temporarily limited.

   o Escalate for legal review – If malicious intent is suspected, HR and legal teams may need to investigate further.

By automating response actions, organizations can prevent security incidents before they escalate into full-blown breaches.

Alex's Journey: Investigating a Potential Data Leak

Alex's company had been using Microsoft Purview for data loss prevention and sensitivity labeling, but leadership wanted to take security a step further by detecting insider risks. The IT team had heard about cases where employees leaked sensitive data to competitors before leaving the company, and they wanted to ensure this didn't happen in their organization.

A few weeks after enabling Insider Risk Management, Purview flagged a high-risk alert. An employee named Chris had downloaded hundreds of confidential files from SharePoint late at night. The system also detected unusual email activity, showing that Chris had sent an encrypted ZIP file to his personal Gmail account.

At first, Alex wasn't sure if this was an accident or a deliberate act, so he reviewed the Purview risk timeline. He noticed that Chris had also recently submitted his resignation notice. This raised a red flag—employees leaving the company often try to take valuable data with them.

Alex escalated the issue to HR and legal teams, and after further review, they confirmed that Chris had violated company policy. His access to sensitive files was immediately revoked, and IT placed a hold on his account to prevent further data transfers. Because the organization had a security policy in place, they were able to recover the data before it left the company.

After the incident, Alex worked with leadership to tighten insider risk policies, ensuring that all departing employees had restricted access to confidential information during their final weeks.

Insider risks are among the most challenging security threats to manage because they involve trusted users with legitimate access. Whether caused by negligence or malicious intent, insider threats can lead to data leaks, financial losses, and compliance violations.

Microsoft Purview helps organizations proactively detect risky behavior and prevent data breaches before they happen. By setting up customized risk policies, monitoring user activity, and automating security responses, organizations can strengthen their data protection strategy without disrupting employee productivity.

For Alex, implementing Insider Risk Management was a critical step in securing his company's sensitive information. But his security journey wasn't over yet. His next challenge was ensuring regulatory compliance and audit readiness—a task that required mastering Microsoft Purview's compliance management tools.

CHAPTER 6: USING MICROSOFT PURVIEW FOR COMPLIANCE AND AUDITING

For many organizations, security isn't just about protecting data from cyber threats—it's also about meeting regulatory requirements and proving compliance. Governments and industry regulators impose strict rules to ensure that companies handle sensitive data responsibly. Failing to comply with these regulations can result in legal consequences, financial penalties, and reputational damage.

Managing compliance, however, can be complex. Organizations must continuously track who accesses data, how it is shared, and whether security policies align with regulatory standards. This process becomes even more challenging in industries like healthcare, finance, and government, where compliance laws are constantly evolving.

Microsoft Purview simplifies this process by providing a centralized Compliance Manager and Audit Logging tools that help organizations track compliance status, generate reports, and respond to audits efficiently. Instead of relying on manual compliance tracking, security teams can automate compliance monitoring and quickly identify gaps in their security policies.

Regulations such as GDPR, HIPAA, NIST, and SOX require organizations to enforce strict data protection policies, auditing practices, and access controls. The challenge for many companies is not only meeting these regulations but also being able to prove compliance during an audit.

Microsoft Purview provides organizations with a structured approach to regulatory compliance by:

- Monitoring compliance in real-time and identifying security gaps

- Generating compliance reports to simplify audit preparation
- Tracking all data access and security incidents for legal and forensic investigations
- Automating risk assessments to help security teams stay ahead of compliance violations

Instead of treating compliance as a reactive process, organizations can use Purview to proactively align security policies with regulatory requirements.

Microsoft Purview Compliance Manager is a built-in tool that provides organizations with a comprehensive compliance dashboard. It allows security teams to:

- Assess their current compliance status with regulations such as GDPR, HIPAA, and ISO 27001
- Receive recommendations for improving compliance based on Microsoft's best practices
- Track ongoing compliance tasks and assign remediation actions to different teams
- Generate detailed reports that auditors and regulatory bodies require

When an organization first accesses Compliance Manager, it provides a compliance score based on how well the company meets regulatory requirements. This score is broken down into different security categories, including data protection, risk management, and access control policies.

For example, if an organization is subject to HIPAA regulations, Compliance Manager might flag that email encryption is not enabled for messages containing patient health records. It would then provide step-by-step guidance on how to remediate the issue to align with HIPAA standards.

By using Compliance Manager, security teams can quickly identify gaps in compliance and take corrective action before an audit takes place.

A critical part of maintaining compliance is having detailed records of all security activities. If an organization experiences a security incident, it must be able to track who accessed sensitive files, when they were accessed, and what actions were taken.

Microsoft Purview's Audit Logging tool allows organizations to:

- Monitor all user activities related to data access, file sharing, and email communication

- Investigate potential security incidents by reviewing detailed logs of suspicious behavior

- Ensure regulatory compliance by generating reports that prove data access policies are enforced

For example, if a financial institution is audited for SOX compliance, regulators may ask for logs showing all administrator access to financial reports over the past six months. Instead of manually searching through fragmented records, the IT team can use Purview's audit search feature to quickly generate a detailed activity report.

Security teams can also configure real-time alerts to detect unusual behavior, such as:

- A user downloading large volumes of confidential data

- An administrator making unauthorized changes to security policies

- A departing employee forwarding company emails to a personal account

By proactively monitoring audit logs, organizations can prevent compliance violations before they become major security risks.

Beyond tracking compliance and auditing activities, Microsoft Purview helps organizations implement strong data governance policies to ensure that security policies remain effective.

Some best practices for maintaining compliance with Microsoft Purview include:

- Defining clear data classification policies so that employees know how to handle sensitive information

- Setting up automatic retention policies to keep or delete records based on regulatory requirements

- Enforcing least-privilege access controls to limit who can view, edit, and share sensitive data

- Regularly reviewing compliance scores in Compliance Manager to stay ahead of security risks

By combining compliance tracking, auditing tools, and proactive security enforcement, organizations can ensure that they remain compliant with industry regulations while minimizing security risks.

Alex's Journey: Preparing for an Internal Audit Using Purview

As his company grew, Alex knew that compliance would become an increasing priority. Regulations like GDPR and HIPAA required them to track security policies, generate compliance reports, and be prepared for audits at any time.

One day, leadership informed Alex that the company would be undergoing an internal security audit to assess their compliance readiness. The auditors needed reports on:

- Who had accessed sensitive customer data over the past six months

- Whether security policies aligned with regulatory requirements

- What measures were in place to prevent unauthorized data sharing

Alex immediately turned to Microsoft Purview's Compliance Manager to review the company's compliance score. He discovered that while the company had strong data encryption policies in place, they were missing key requirements related to data retention and access logging.

To address these gaps, Alex took the following actions:

- Enabled detailed audit logging for sensitive files and user access activities

- Configured retention policies to ensure compliance with data storage regulations

- Updated access controls so that only authorized employees could view confidential records

After implementing these changes, Alex generated a compliance report directly from Compliance Manager, which provided auditors with a clear summary of the company's security posture.

During the audit, leadership was impressed by how quickly Alex was able to produce reports, track compliance status, and demonstrate security controls. Instead of scrambling to gather evidence manually, everything was automated and accessible within Microsoft Purview.

The audit was successful, and the company's security team gained new insights into areas for future improvement. Alex also set up a quarterly compliance review process to ensure that security policies remained aligned with evolving regulations.

Regulatory compliance is no longer an optional task—it is a critical business requirement. Organizations must ensure that they not only enforce security policies but also have the ability to prove compliance when required.

Microsoft Purview simplifies compliance management by automating risk assessments, tracking security activities, and generating audit-ready reports. Instead of waiting for auditors to highlight security gaps, organizations can use Compliance Manager to proactively improve their security posture.

For Alex, mastering compliance tools meant that his company could confidently handle audits, meet regulatory requirements, and reduce legal risks. But he also knew that security threats were always evolving. His next challenge was to explore how AI and automation could enhance security operations—an area where Microsoft Security Copilot would play a major role.

CHAPTER 7: AUTOMATING SECURITY WITH AI AND MICROSOFT SECURITY COPILOT

Cybersecurity threats are increasing in both complexity and frequency, making it nearly impossible for human security teams to keep up using traditional tools alone. Attackers are using more advanced tactics, from social engineering to AI-driven attacks, and organizations must respond with equally intelligent defenses. Security professionals already deal with a constant flood of alerts, log files, and compliance reports. Manually reviewing and investigating each security event is not only inefficient but also leaves room for human error.

This is where artificial intelligence is changing the game. AI-driven security automation allows organizations to move from reactive security measures to proactive threat detection and prevention. Instead of responding to incidents after they occur, security teams can anticipate and block threats before they cause damage. AI also reduces the burden of manual tasks by analyzing security data in real time, identifying patterns that indicate risk, and recommending immediate actions to mitigate potential breaches.

Microsoft Security Copilot is one of the most powerful AI-driven security tools available today. It integrates with Microsoft Purview, Microsoft Defender, and other security solutions to provide real-time insights, automate response actions, and simplify compliance tracking. Instead of relying on human analysts to sift through thousands of logs, Security Copilot can summarize key security events, highlight areas of concern, and even suggest remediation steps.

One of the biggest challenges in cybersecurity is differentiating between normal user behavior and suspicious activity. Traditional security systems rely on static rules—for example, blocking logins from unknown locations or restricting file downloads over a certain limit. The problem with this approach is that it often results in too many false positives or, worse, misses subtle threats that don't fit a predefined pattern. AI-driven security works differently. It learns from user behavior over time, allowing it to distinguish between routine activity and true anomalies.

For example, if an employee typically logs in from Chicago during work hours but suddenly accesses sensitive files from another country at midnight, Security Copilot can recognize this as abnormal behavior. But rather than immediately blocking access, it analyzes additional factors— such as whether the user is using a known device, whether their location data fluctuates frequently, and whether similar incidents have been flagged in the past. Based on this analysis, it determines whether an alert should be raised, whether access should be temporarily blocked, or whether additional authentication is required. This level of intelligence reduces unnecessary disruptions while ensuring real security threats are addressed quickly.

AI is also transforming how organizations handle compliance and security governance. Many industries, including finance, healthcare, and government, are subject to strict regulatory requirements such as GDPR, HIPAA, and NIST. Maintaining compliance requires constant monitoring of security policies, data access controls, and incident response protocols. Security teams traditionally spend significant time conducting audits, generating reports, and ensuring that security measures align with legal requirements. Security Copilot can automate much of this process by continuously scanning an organization's security environment, identifying areas of non-compliance, and suggesting remediation steps. Instead of manually compiling compliance reports, organizations can generate them in real time, allowing for faster and more efficient audits.

AI also plays a crucial role in incident response. When a security breach occurs, every second matters. A slow response can mean greater data exposure, financial losses, and reputational damage. Traditional security operations require analysts to manually investigate alerts, correlate security logs, and determine the severity of a breach before taking action.

Security Copilot accelerates this process by automatically identifying the scope of an incident, analyzing its impact, and suggesting response actions. In some cases, it can even take action autonomously, such as isolating a compromised device or blocking a suspicious login attempt.

AI-driven security is already proving its value in real-world scenarios. In the financial sector, AI models help detect fraudulent transactions by analyzing spending patterns and transaction behaviors that would be impossible for a human analyst to process manually. In healthcare, AI systems help monitor and restrict access to patient records, ensuring compliance with privacy laws while preventing unauthorized access. Large enterprises use AI-powered security to prevent insider threats, identifying unusual data access behaviors that could indicate an employee preparing to leave the company with confidential information.

Alex's Journey: Leveraging AI Insights to Improve Security Posture

After implementing Microsoft Purview's compliance and data protection tools, Alex's company faced a new challenge: the growing volume of security alerts. His IT team was stretched thin, spending hours investigating potential threats, many of which turned out to be false alarms. Recognizing the need for a more efficient approach, Alex turned to Microsoft Security Copilot.

One of the first incidents where AI proved its value was a series of unusual login attempts from an employee's account at odd hours. In the past, investigating such an event would have required combing through logs and manually verifying the details. Security Copilot, however, instantly provided an analysis of the situation, correlating it with past behavior and determining whether similar activity had been flagged before. It took into account not just the time of login but also the device used, the location, and whether this kind of access had been previously marked as suspicious. Based on this insight, Alex was able to take immediate action, resetting the user's credentials and enforcing additional authentication measures.

Another major breakthrough came when Security Copilot detected a phishing attempt targeting the finance department. A well-crafted email requested an urgent wire transfer, appearing to come from a trusted vendor. On the surface, the message looked legitimate—no obvious misspellings or formatting errors that would typically mark it as suspicious. Before an employee could act on it, Security Copilot compared the sender's email address against past interactions, analyzed the tone and urgency of the message, and cross-referenced it with known phishing tactics. Within seconds, it flagged the message as suspicious, quarantined it, and alerted Alex's team for further review.

As Alex continued using Security Copilot, he noticed another unexpected benefit: AI was helping his team connect the dots between seemingly unrelated security events. In one case, a departing employee had recently submitted their resignation notice. Around the same time, an alert came through about unusual file downloads from that employee's account. Rather than treating the two incidents separately, Security Copilot identified a pattern—departing employees are statistically more likely to engage in data exfiltration. With this insight, Alex's team quickly reviewed the employee's activities, confirmed that the downloaded files contained proprietary company information, and acted before the data could be transferred externally.

Beyond threat detection, Alex also began using Security Copilot to strengthen compliance efforts. His company was preparing for an external audit, and instead of manually gathering compliance reports and policy enforcement details, he leveraged AI-driven insights to automate compliance checks. Security Copilot generated real-time assessments of policy adherence, flagged areas that required attention, and even provided remediation steps. What previously took days of effort was now completed in hours, allowing Alex to focus on strategic improvements rather than administrative tasks.

Over time, AI became an indispensable part of Alex's security strategy. Instead of reacting to threats after they had already escalated, his team was now able to prevent security incidents before they happened. Security Copilot reduced false positives, streamlined compliance tracking, and provided intelligent recommendations that allowed them to work smarter, not harder. It wasn't just a tool—it became a force multiplier, enhancing every aspect of security and compliance in the organization.

For Alex, this shift reinforced an important lesson: securing an organization isn't just about having the right tools—it's about leveraging technology to create a proactive, resilient security posture. AI had given his team the insights and automation they needed to stay ahead of threats, allowing them to focus on more strategic initiatives rather than constantly playing defense. What started as a way to manage alerts had become a game-changer, transforming how his company approached security at every level.

CHAPTER 8: DATA SECURITY BEST PRACTICES FOR ORGANIZATIONS

Securing an organization's data is not just about deploying the right tools—it requires a comprehensive approach that combines technology, policies, and people. Even with Microsoft Purview, Microsoft Defender, and AI-powered security automation, an organization's security posture is only as strong as its weakest link. Employees can still fall for phishing scams, misconfigure security settings, or unknowingly share sensitive data. That's why establishing strong security policies, training employees, and continuously improving security strategies are essential for long-term data protection.

Effective data security is a continuous process. Threats evolve, compliance regulations change, and organizations must adapt to stay ahead. Security leaders need to move beyond reactive security and adopt proactive strategies that prevent security incidents before they happen. A key part of this is ensuring that Microsoft Purview is aligned with a Zero Trust security model, where organizations assume that no user, device, or application should be trusted by default.

By establishing best practices in security policy development, employee education, and ongoing security monitoring, organizations can reduce risk and create a security-first culture that prioritizes data protection at every level.

A strong security policy framework is the foundation of any organization's data protection strategy. These policies should clearly define how sensitive data is classified, stored, accessed, and shared. Policies must also specify security requirements for user authentication, device management, and network access. Without well-defined rules, security risks increase as employees may handle sensitive data inconsistently.

Security policies should cover key areas such as:

- Data classification: Establishing categories for sensitive information such as internal documents, financial records, or personally identifiable information (PII).

- Access control: Defining who can access, edit, or share specific types of data and under what conditions.

- Incident response: Outlining how the organization responds to security breaches, including reporting and remediation steps.

- Encryption standards: Ensuring that data is encrypted both in transit and at rest, reducing exposure to data leaks.

However, policies alone are not enough. Employees need to be trained on why these policies exist and how to follow them. Many security incidents result from human error rather than malicious intent, meaning that proper training can significantly reduce risk. Employees should be educated on topics such as phishing awareness, password security, and safe data-sharing practices.

Microsoft Purview helps enforce these policies by integrating Data Loss Prevention (DLP), Sensitivity Labels, and Insider Risk Management. But technology can only do so much. Organizations must invest in ongoing security training to ensure that employees understand their role in protecting sensitive data.

One of the most effective ways to strengthen an organization's security posture is to align Microsoft Purview with a Zero Trust security model. Traditional security strategies rely on perimeter-based protection— assuming that everything inside an organization's network is safe. But in a world of cloud computing, remote work, and bring-your-own-device (BYOD) policies, this assumption no longer holds true.

Zero Trust security operates on the principle of "Never trust, always verify." It assumes that threats can exist both inside and outside an organization's network, and therefore, every user, device, and application must continuously prove their legitimacy before gaining access to sensitive resources.

To integrate Purview with a Zero Trust approach, organizations should:

- Implement multi-factor authentication (MFA): Ensure that user identities are verified through multiple authentication factors before granting access.

- Use conditional access policies: Restrict access based on factors such as user role, device security posture, and geographic location.

- Limit user privileges: Apply the least privilege principle, meaning that employees only have access to the data necessary for their job.

- Monitor all access and activity: Continuously track who is accessing what data, when, and from where using Microsoft Purview's audit logs and Insider Risk Management tools.

By combining Microsoft Purview's data protection features with Zero Trust security, organizations create an environment where security is continuously enforced, reducing the risk of unauthorized access and data leaks.

Security is not a "set it and forget it" process. Organizations must continuously monitor their security environment and adjust policies as threats evolve. Cybercriminals are constantly finding new ways to bypass security measures, making regular assessments and proactive improvements necessary.

Ongoing security monitoring should include:

- Regular security audits: Conduct periodic compliance reviews using Microsoft Purview's Compliance Manager to ensure adherence to industry regulations.

- Threat intelligence analysis: Use Microsoft Defender and Security Copilot to analyze emerging cybersecurity threats and adjust security policies accordingly.

- Incident response testing: Simulate security breaches to evaluate the effectiveness of data protection policies, response procedures, and employee readiness.

- Feedback loops: Encourage employees and IT teams to report potential security gaps and continuously improve security training programs.

By taking a proactive approach to security, organizations stay ahead of evolving threats and ensure that their data security strategy remains effective.

Alex's Journey: Building a Security Roadmap for His Company

After successfully implementing Microsoft Purview's data protection and compliance tools, Alex realized that security is an ongoing process, not a one-time project. While his team had set up Data Loss Prevention, Insider Risk Management, and AI-driven security automation, there was still work to be done in creating a long-term security roadmap.

One of the first areas Alex focused on was improving employee awareness of security policies. His company had suffered a near miss when an employee nearly fell for a phishing attack, but security tools intervened before any data was exposed. To prevent future incidents, Alex worked with HR to launch a company-wide security training initiative. Employees were required to complete phishing awareness exercises and participate in hands-on security workshops to reinforce safe data handling practices.

Alex also worked to align his company's Microsoft Purview implementation with a Zero Trust security model. He realized that while their data classification and access control policies were strong, there were still gaps in identity and device security. He collaborated with IT to:

- Enforce multi-factor authentication for all employees
- Restrict access to sensitive files based on job roles
- Enable conditional access policies that blocked risky sign-in attempts

The biggest challenge Alex faced was convincing leadership that continuous monitoring was necessary. Some executives were skeptical about the need for ongoing security assessments, believing that their initial setup was enough. To address these concerns, Alex presented a report generated by Microsoft Purview's Compliance Manager, showing where security gaps still existed and how the organization compared to industry standards. This helped leadership understand that security wasn't just about preventing external attacks, but also about ensuring regulatory compliance and protecting company data from accidental leaks.

As part of his long-term strategy, Alex scheduled quarterly security audits, phishing simulations, and compliance check-ins. By integrating real-time monitoring, AI-driven threat detection, and employee training, his company transitioned from reactive security to a proactive, Zero Trust security model.

Over time, Alex saw a measurable improvement in his company's security posture. Data incidents decreased, employees became more security-conscious, and compliance scores improved. More importantly, security became part of the company's culture rather than an afterthought.

Looking back, Alex realized that data security is not just about having the right tools—it's about building a sustainable security strategy that adapts to new threats. Microsoft Purview gave him the framework to protect his company's data, but it was the ongoing policies, training, and security roadmap that made the biggest impact.

Data security is an ongoing journey that requires the right mix of technology, policies, and education. Organizations that invest in strong security practices, employee training, and continuous monitoring are far better positioned to prevent breaches, maintain compliance, and safeguard their most valuable data.

By implementing Microsoft Purview's data security features, aligning with Zero Trust principles, and committing to continuous security improvements, companies can stay ahead of evolving threats and create a lasting security culture.

MASTERING DATA SECURITY WITH MICROSOFT PURVIEW

Securing an organization's data is no longer a luxury—it's a necessity. As cyber threats grow more sophisticated, businesses of all sizes must adopt a comprehensive, proactive approach to data security and compliance. Microsoft Purview provides the tools needed to classify, protect, monitor, and govern data, but the key to success lies in how organizations implement and maintain their security strategies over time.

This book has explored the fundamental concepts of Microsoft Purview, from sensitivity labels and data loss prevention to insider risk management and AI-powered security automation. By now, it should be clear that data security is not just about technology—it requires well-defined policies, ongoing monitoring, and a security-first culture.

Organizations that successfully implement Microsoft Purview gain a stronger security posture, improved compliance alignment, and greater visibility into how data is used and shared. But even with the best tools, security is an ongoing journey. Threats evolve, compliance requirements shift, and businesses must continuously refine their security strategies to stay ahead.

Looking back at the topics covered, a few key lessons stand out:

- Data security starts with classification. Organizations must understand their data, categorize it based on sensitivity, and apply protection policies accordingly. Microsoft Purview's sensitivity labels and data classification tools help automate this process.

- Preventing data loss requires a balance of technology and policy. Data Loss Prevention (DLP) policies are essential for controlling how sensitive data is shared and stored. But technology alone isn't enough—organizations need clear policies and employee training to ensure data protection is followed at every level.

- Insider threats are just as dangerous as external attacks. Employees, whether accidentally or intentionally, can pose significant security risks. Microsoft Purview's Insider Risk Management helps detect suspicious activities, enforce access controls, and mitigate risks before they escalate.

- AI-powered security is the future of threat detection. Microsoft Security Copilot enhances security operations by automating threat analysis, reducing false positives, and providing real-time security insights. AI-driven security ensures faster responses to potential breaches, helping organizations stay ahead of cybercriminals.

- Compliance isn't just a checkbox—it's a continuous process. Regulations like GDPR, HIPAA, and NIST require organizations to regularly assess their security posture and ensure they meet compliance standards. Microsoft Purview's Compliance Manager simplifies this process by providing real-time assessments and remediation steps.

- Zero Trust security should be the foundation of every organization's data strategy. The old approach of trusting everything inside the corporate network is no longer sufficient. Organizations must adopt a "never trust, always verify" mindset by implementing multi-factor authentication, conditional access, and least privilege access controls.

By following these principles, organizations can not only protect their data but also build a security culture that adapts to new threats and compliance requirements.

For organizations looking to take their Microsoft Purview implementation to the next level, there are several advanced features and certifications that can enhance security and compliance efforts.

- Microsoft Purview Advanced eDiscovery provides legal teams with enhanced tools for managing compliance investigations, litigation requests, and forensic data analysis. This is essential for organizations that need to respond to legal requests quickly and efficiently.

- Microsoft Purview Customer Lockbox adds an extra layer of control over Microsoft support access to sensitive data. This is particularly useful for industries with strict compliance requirements, such as healthcare and finance.

- Microsoft Purview Advanced Audit extends audit log retention and provides deeper forensic analysis of user activity. For companies that require detailed security investigations and compliance reporting, this tool is a powerful addition.

For IT professionals looking to validate their expertise, Microsoft offers certifications that cover security, compliance, and risk management in Microsoft 365 and Purview. Some of the most relevant certifications include:

- Microsoft Certified: Security, Compliance, and Identity Fundamentals (SC-900) – A great starting point for those new to security and compliance.

- Microsoft Certified: Information Protection Administrator Associate (SC-400) – A more advanced certification for professionals managing data security, compliance, and governance policies.

- Microsoft Certified: Cybersecurity Architect Expert (SC-100) – Designed for those leading enterprise security strategies, including Zero Trust frameworks.

By pursuing these advanced features and certifications, organizations and IT professionals can stay ahead of evolving security challenges and maximize the value of their Microsoft Purview investment.

Final Reflections from Alex on His Purview Journey

After months of implementing Microsoft Purview, refining security policies, and enhancing his company's overall security strategy, Alex took a step back to evaluate the progress his team had made. What started as a response to increasing security threats and compliance challenges had evolved into a company-wide transformation.

At the beginning of the journey, security incidents were a constant concern. Data was being shared without proper oversight, compliance audits were stressful and time-consuming, and the IT team felt overwhelmed by the number of security alerts they had to investigate manually.

With Microsoft Purview fully implemented, Alex saw a dramatic improvement in security operations.

- Data classification and sensitivity labels ensured that confidential information was protected automatically. Employees no longer had to guess whether data was safe to share—Purview's built-in policies handled it for them.

- Data Loss Prevention (DLP) significantly reduced the risk of accidental data exposure. Files containing sensitive financial or HR data could no longer be emailed to personal accounts or shared outside the organization without proper authorization.

- Insider Risk Management helped the team detect and prevent potential data exfiltration. Instead of reacting after a data breach, they were now able to intervene before security incidents could cause harm.

- AI-powered security automation transformed how security incidents were handled. Security Copilot's ability to analyze threats and suggest remediation steps meant that IT could focus on high-priority security issues rather than wasting time on false positives.

- Regulatory compliance became an ongoing, automated process rather than a last-minute scramble before an audit. Compliance

Manager continuously assessed how well the organization met GDPR, HIPAA, and NIST standards, providing clear recommendations for improvement.

- A Zero Trust security model was fully integrated into the organization's security strategy. Access to sensitive data was strictly controlled, multi-factor authentication was enforced for all employees, and conditional access policies helped prevent unauthorized logins.

But beyond all of the technical improvements, Alex noticed a cultural shift within his organization. Security was no longer just an IT concern—it had become a shared responsibility across all departments. Employees understood the importance of protecting company data, following security policies, and reporting suspicious activity. Leadership no longer saw compliance as an obstacle, but as a necessary investment in the company's long-term success.

Reflecting on everything he had learned, Alex realized that security wasn't just about having the best tools—it was about creating a sustainable security strategy. Microsoft Purview had provided the foundation, but it was the combination of technology, policy enforcement, ongoing training, and a proactive mindset that made the real difference.

Looking ahead, Alex knew that cyber threats would continue to evolve, and compliance requirements would change. But he felt confident that with Microsoft Purview, AI-driven security automation, and a Zero Trust approach, his organization was better prepared than ever to handle the challenges of modern data security.

Mastering data security with Microsoft Purview is not about checking boxes or implementing tools once—it's about building a security-first culture. The organizations that succeed in data protection are those that continuously assess, refine, and adapt their security strategies to meet evolving threats.

For security professionals and IT leaders, the journey doesn't end here. Staying ahead requires ongoing learning, leveraging advanced features, and maintaining a proactive mindset. By doing so, businesses can protect their most valuable asset—their data—while ensuring trust, compliance, and security for the future.

www.ingramcontent.com/pod-product-compliance
Lightning Source LLC
LaVergne TN
LVHW051616050326
832903LV00033B/4520